Louis FitzGerald Benson

Hymns and Verses

Louis FitzGerald Benson

Hymns and Verses

ISBN/EAN: 9783337075989

Printed in Europe, USA, Canada, Australia, Japan

Cover: Foto ©Thomas Meinert / pixelio.de

More available books at **www.hansebooks.com**

Hymns & Verses

By

Louis F. Benson

Philadelphia
The Westminster Press
MDCCCXCVII

To

C. P. B.

Take my book, my lady,
   In your gracious hand:
But a look, my lady,
As you turn its pages over;
And a smile to tell your lover
     That you care and understand!
Take your book, my lady;
   May I kiss your hand?

Take my heart, my lady;
   Let me keep your hand:
From the start, my lady,
It has always been June weather
As we came this way together
     In the light that filled the land.
Keep my heart, my lady;
   May I keep your hand?

Contents

HYMNS

Happy Town of Salem	Page 11
A Morning Hymn of Praise	14
At Lauds	16
Beyond Life's Evening Star	18
The Law of God	20
The Lord of Glory	22
A Morning Hymn	24
A Communion Hymn	26
A Hymn of Faith	28
In His Presence	30
Christ and His Church	32
Before the Cross	34
A College Hymn	36
"It is Finished!"	38
The Summons of the Sea	40
When We Came Back to Love	42
At the Installation of a Pastor	44
At the Opening of Service	46
Offertory	48
At the Close of Service	49

Contents

HYMNS FROM THE LATIN

O Luce Qui Mortalibus	Page 53
O Christe, Qui Noster Poli	56
Crux Ave Benedicta!	58
Nobis, Olympo Redditus	60
Ter Sancte, Ter Potens Deus	62
Nil Laudibus Nostris Eges	64
O Pater Sancte Mitis Atque Pie	66
Deus, Pater Ingenite	68
Salvator Mundi, Domine	70

VERSES

The Bells of Christ Church	75
Little Foot on the Fender	77
The Last Hill	78
On Lake George	81
My Father's House	82
"And There Shall Be No Night There"	84
An Auction	86
An Afternoon in November	88
The Praise of Penn	90
Memory	93
Familiar Music	94

Contents

THE OLD LOVES AND THE NEW	*Page* 96
A NOONING	98
TO-MORROW	99
THE TEMPLE OF THE NEW JERUSALEM	100

SONNETS

BRYANT	107
A DEDICATION	108
LONELINESS	109
THE UNCHANGEABLE	110
CEDARS BY MOONLIGHT	111
OF THEM THAT SLEEP	112

THE MARCH OF BRADDOCK	115

Hymns

HAPPY TOWN OF SALEM

*" Urbs beata Ierusalem
Dicta pacis visio."*

I

HAPPY town of Salem,
   Set on Zion's hill!
Happy hearts of pilgrims,
   Could they see it still!
He that follows Jesus,
   He that dares the right,
Sees the lights of Salem
   Gleam across the night.

II

Happy town of Salem,
   With the jasper wall!
In its many mansions
   There is room for all.
"Come to Me," says Jesus,
   "I will give you rest;"
And the town of Salem
   Gathers all the blest.

Happy Town of Salem

III

Happy town of Salem!
   Happy little feet
Of the children playing
   In the golden street!
"Let them come," says Jesus,
   "And forbid them not;"
But the proud in Salem
   Have no part nor lot.

IV

Happy town of Salem,
   With its open gates!
Happy are the pilgrims
   Whom a welcome waits!
In the Name of Jesus
   They an entrance claim,
And the guards of Salem
   Answer, "In His Name."

V

Happy town of Salem,
   Vision true of peace,
Seen above earth's strivings,
   Steadfast when they cease!

Happy Town of Salem

"Take thy cross," says Jesus;
  And the narrow way
Brings the feet to Salem
  At the break of day.

A MORNING HYMN OF PRAISE

I

THE sun is on the land and sea,
    The day begun;
Our morning hymn begins with Thee,
    Blest Three-in-One:
Our praise shall rise continuously
    Till day is done.

II

Thy love was ever in our view,
    Like stars, by night;
Thy gifts are every morning new,
    O God of light;
Thy mercy, like the heavens' blue,
    Fills all our sight.

III

We do not know what grief or care
    The day may bring:

A Morning Hymn of Praise

The heart shall find some gladness there
   That loves its King;
The life that serves Thee everywhere
   Can always sing.

IV

All glory to the Father be,
   With Christ the Son,
And, Holy Spirit, unto Thee,
   Forever One;
All glory to the Trinity
   While ages run.

AT LAUDS

I

Our King's own child, the morning,
    Uplifts its golden head;
The gems its crown adorning
    Are pearls and rubies red:
And fleecy stuffs in cloudland made
Are on its shoulders lightly laid.

II

Our King's best gift, the morning,
    Lies lavish o'er the land,
But shrinks within the scorning
    Of an unwilling hand.
Lord, make us wise the best to choose,
And to Thy praise Thy gifts to use.

III

The royal lights of morning,
    How quickly paled and gray!

At Lauds

And falls, with scarce a warning,
　　The light of common day:
Perchance the common day may be
The golden opportunity.

IV

To God, the light's Creator,
　　To Christ, the Light of Light,
To God, Illuminator,
　　Be praise from dawn to night.
To God, enthroned above the skies,
Our morning song shall ever rise.

BEYOND LIFE'S EVENING STAR

I

Good Shepherd! Theirs, who heard Thy call;
  Content to walk with Thee,
While sunlight stays, when shadows fall,
  And then — we could not see —
    Beyond life's evening star,
      Into the paling west,
    Where they who followed far
      Have ended now their quest.

II

Good Shepherd! Ours, with feet less bold
  To choose the way they took;
Half longing for that distant fold,
  And half afraid to look
    Beyond life's evening star,
      Beyond the things that seem,
    Nor shade nor sunlight are, —
      The twilight and the dream!

Beyond Life's Evening Star

III

Good Shepherd! When we leave Thy side
  In doubtful dreams to stray,
Our wayward eyes refuse their Guide,
  Who only knows the way
    Beyond life's evening star
      And through the paling west,
    Where they who follow far
      Are with Thee still in rest.

THE LAW OF GOD

I

THY laws, O God, forever steadfast stand
    Till all shall be fulfilled;
The sceptre is not fallen from Thy hand,
    Nor Sinai's trumpet stilled.

II

O Thou whose voice proclaims Thy changeless will,
    Imperial as Thy grace,
Who shall ascend unto Thy holy hill,
    And stand before Thy face?

III

No strength of soul can that clear height attain,
    Nor pride for sin atone;
And sacrifice uplifts its hands in vain
    To plead at Mercy's throne.

The Law of God

IV

But he whose hands, O Christ, are brotherly,
   And, like Thine own, are just;
Whose feet through lowly ways have walked with
      Thee
   In humble, child-like trust;

V

He shall ascend unto Thy holy hill,
   And dwell with Thee above;
For, though Thy statutes are imperious still,
   Thy law, O God, is love.

THE LORD OF GLORY

I

A GLORY lit the wintry sky
    Before the break of day,
And in a little house near by
    The Lord of Glory lay:
        Angels of peace the tidings bring,
        Angels of Jesus sing.

II

Our common ways with anxious feet
    The Lord of Glory trod,
But met not one in lane or street
    That knew the Son of God:
        Angels of peace their greetings bring,
        Angels that may not sing.

III

"I come to bring the weary rest,"
    The Lord of Glory said,

The Lord of Glory

Yet found no place to east or west
  Where He might lay His head:
    Angels of peace above Him still,
    Angels await His will.

IV

And when they led Him forth to die,
  Around His cross of shame
The men He came to save stood by
  And mocked their Saviour's Name:
    Angels of peace their stations keep,
    Angels of sorrow weep.

V

O Son of Man whom angels know!
  O heart of man, how cold,
How dull to see, to praise how slow,
  Now as in days of old!
    Angels of peace their hymns upraise,
    Angels of glory praise.

A MORNING HYMN

I

WHEN I awake from slumber
   To greet the golden day,
Then teach me, Lord, to number
   Its hours in wisdom's way.

II

When clouds at dawn are gleaming,
   Lift up mine answering eyes
To where Thy light is streaming
   On faith's high enterprise.

III

Whither I hear Thee calling,
   Lord, give me grace to run;
Keep Thou my feet from falling
   Until Thy will is done.

A Morning Hymn

IV

Whene'er the heart grows weary,
   And every goal seems far,
Reveal Thyself as near me
   As life and duty are.

V

And when the light is fading,
   If dreams have not come true,
Yet may Thy peace pervading
   Be breathed the twilight through.

VI

When day at last is ended,
   And shadows are grown deep,
By Thy kind arms defended,
   Lord, lay me down to sleep.

A COMMUNION HYMN

I

LO! Thou art with us, Lord,
    Now, always, to the end.
Why stand we gazing heavenward
    To find Thee, nearest Friend?

II

Lo! Thou art with us, Lord;
    Of every heart the Guest,
The Bond which binds in sweet accord
    All hearts that in Thee rest.

III

Lo! Thou art with us, Lord;
    Of Thine own House the Head,
Thou sittest at the holy board
    To bless the broken bread.

A Communion Hymn

IV

Lo! Thou art with us, Lord,
   Who still Thyself dost give;
Thy life the cup which is outpoured,
   The bread by which we live.

V

Lo! Thou art with us, Lord,
   Whom Thou hast never failed;
Here where Thy presence is adored,
   Thy face but thinly veiled.

A HYMN OF FAITH

I

WE would not climb with earth-bound feet
   High airy ways untrod,
Where angels, hither coming, meet
   Those going back to God:
We would not strain our wearied eyes
   To see the paths they took,
Nor blind them in the light that lies
   Where angels fear to look.

II

We have not sought with human span
   To measure ways like Thine,
Nor dreamed, O God, that mortal man
   Could think Thy thoughts Divine:
In vain our futile patience waits
   Till knowledge turns the key
That opens wide the sealèd gates
   Of Thine infinity.

A Hymn of Faith

III

And yet, as high as faith may go,
   As far as knowledge see,
The heart would seek its Lord to know,
   The mind discover Thee:
Would know Thee, unto truth drawn nigh
   By loving what is true;
Would see Thee, as the climber's eye
   Anticipates the view.

IV

We rest upon Thy fatherhood,
   While, round and overhead,
Thy being's boundless amplitude
   Like seas and sky is spread.
Oh, better than in vain to try
   To plumb th' unsounded sea,
Or win the secrets of the sky,
   It is to rest in Thee.

IN HIS PRESENCE

I

All life is in Thy presence, Lord;
   Our deeds are in Thy sight;
Thine eyes behold, Thy hands record
   Our very thoughts by night.

II

All life is in Thy presence, Lord;
   And, hallowed by Thy smile,
Its humblest tasks great hopes afford,
   Its failures seem worth while.

III

All life is in Thy presence, Lord;
   And most that life is blest
Which finds Thy favor its reward,
   And Thy protection rest.

In His Presence

IV

All life is in Thy presence, Lord;
   Content to dwell with Thee
When by Thy fellowship restored
   To peace and purity.

V

All life is in Thy presence, Lord;
   By all things, great and small,
Be Thy blest Name Triune adored,
   Who art the All-in-all.

CHRIST AND HIS CHURCH

I

THINE eyes sought out Thine own,
  Thy voice said, "Follow Me;"
To simple hearts of Galilee
Thy light and love were shown.
    O Jesus, we are Thine,
      Thou callest us to-day;
    Thy light and love still steadfast shine
      To guide Thy Church's way.

II

Thine eyes among Thy flock
  For living faith made search;
  Thy voice exulting said, "My Church
I build upon this rock."
    O Jesus, guard it well,
      Lest faith and courage fail;
    Thou wilt not let the gates of hell
      Against Thy Church prevail.

Christ and His Church

III

Thine eyes saw, full in view,
  Thy cross stand just ahead;
  Thy voice to Thine eleven said,
"My peace I leave with you."
    O Jesus, at Thy side
      All strife and discord cease;
    And where her Lord was crucified
      Thy Church shall find her peace.

IV

Thine eyes far glories fill,
  Thy love does not forget;
  Thy voice, where doubting hearts were met,
Said, "I am with you still."
    O Jesus, only Thou,
      Uplifted from the dead
    And throned in highest Heaven now,
      Shalt be Thy Church's Head.

BEFORE THE CROSS

I

O HEAVENLY love that was so high,
   So lowly now for love of me!
The Son of God hath stooped to die
   The death of shame upon the tree.
For me the Lord that loved me died;
The Son of God is crucified.

II

The Son of God, the Lord of Life;
   That royal head uncrowned for me!
The Prince of Peace amid the strife;
   His lifted cross my victory!
Here weep, my sin; here kneel, my pride;
The Son of God is crucified.

III

Is crucified! Those hands impaled
   The sins of other hands to bear;

Before the Cross

Those feet, for feet that wandered, nailed;
  For my transgressions wounded there.
For me the Lord that loved me died;
The Son of God is crucified.

IV

Before His cross the heart is hushed,
  The eyes that see their Lord grow dim;
And all the works of pride lie crushed
  Beneath the weight it laid on Him.
No thought, no prayer, no plea, beside
"The Son of God is crucified."

A COLLEGE HYMN

I

O CHRIST, who didst our tasks fulfil,
    Didst share the hopes of youth,
Our Teacher and our Brother still,
    Now lead us into truth.

II

The call is Thine: be Thou the Way,
    And Thine the hearts that guide;
Let wisdom broaden with the day,
    Let human faith abide.

III

Who learns of Thee the truth shall find,
    Who follows, wins the goal;
With reverence crown the earnest mind,
    And speak within the soul.

A College Hymn

IV

Waken the purpose high which strives,
   And, falling, stands again;
Confirm the will of eager lives
   To quit themselves like men:

V

Thy life the bond of fellowship,
   Thy love the law that rules,
Thy Name, proclaimed by every lip,
   The Master of our schools.

"IT IS FINISHED!"

I

"It is finished!" Jesus cries,
As upon the cross He dies.
"It is finished!" says the Son,
For the Father's will is done.

II

"It is finished!" Long ago
Prophets saw Messiah's woe:
Now their visions are fulfilled,
And the Sufferer's heart is stilled.

III

"It is finished!" — every throe
Human strength may undergo,
From the infant's cry for breath
To the bitter sting of death.

"It is Finished!"

IV

"It is finished!"—the long way
Through the gloom to break of day;
And the path of sacrifice
Leads at last to Paradise.

V

"It is finished!" Jesus, rest
With the weary and oppressed,
Till the life Thou hast laid down
Shall arise to take its crown.

VI

"It is finished!" Christ, in Thee
Faith shall claim the victory,
By the deeds that Thou hast done
In the battle Thou hast won.

THE SUMMONS OF THE SEA

I

WHY linger yet upon the sand?
    Why hug the sheltered lee?
O heart of mine, wouldst thou withstand
    The summons of the sea?

II

What wider ways that God has planned
    Bode ill, my life, to thee,
If in the hollow of His hand
    He holds the unknown sea?

III

Why dream of breakers on the shore,
    Or reefs thou canst not see?
O life of mine, what needst thou more,
    If Christ thy Pilot be?

The Summons of the Sea

IV

What woe to thee in wind or tide?
My heart, why frightened be
Aboard life's sinking ship, beside
The One who walks the sea?

WHEN WE CAME BACK TO LOVE

I

OUR wilful hearts have gone astray;
    Our feet have wandered far away;
O God, remember not the day
        When we forsook Thy love.

II

O patient Eyes that saw us go!
O careless hearts to grieve Him so!
O feet so swift to leave, so slow
        When we came back to Love!

III

We followed far the wayward will;
Our eyes turned home from every hill;
They found Thee waiting, watching still
        When we came back to Love.

When We Came Back to Love

IV

We found no home to east or west;
We bore no peace within the breast,
Until once more we were at rest
      When we came back to Love.

V

"Our Father!" Hallowed be the Name
That all within Thy house proclaim;
Their prayer and ours at last the same,—
      Thy will be done, O Love.

AT THE INSTALLATION OF A PASTOR

I

O RISEN Christ, who from Thy throne
    Dost rule Thy Church, and hear Thine own,
Now seal by Thine almighty power
The covenants of this sacred hour.

II

Weave Thou Thy life through these new ties:
The light of love that round Thee lies
Circle the shepherd and the sheep,
And all our lives in safety keep.

III

The shepherd's Shepherd only Thou
Canst be: O Christ, walk with him now;
While our weak hands reach up to Thine,
To strengthen his with might Divine.

At the Installation of a Pastor

IV

Thou in whose love Thy Church is blest,
Thy Name alone be here confessed,
By holy lives be glorified,
While here Thy peace shall still abide.

AT THE OPENING OF SERVICE

I

FATHER, once more within Thy Holy Place
   We bring the sins which, kneeling, we confess;
Not worthy yet to look upon Thy face,
   Yet loath to rise until Thy hand doth bless.

II

Father, once more within Thy House of Hope
   We turn from sin to find a glad release:
In Thy forgiveness there is strength to cope
   With all that robs the spirit of Thy peace.

III

Father, once more within Thy House of Prayer
   We kneel before Thee at the open way;
And, leaving both our hopes and burdens there,
   We wait till Thou shalt teach us how to pray.

At the Opening of Service

IV

Father, once more within Thy House of Praise
   We bring our gifts to Thee from whom they came;
We lift our hearts and our hosannas raise
   To welcome Him who cometh in Thy Name.

OFFERTORY

I

WE can but give Thee what is Thine,
    For we have naught beside:
Accept from us, O Love Divine,
    The gifts Thou dost provide.

II

To whom, O Saviour, but to Thee,
    Must cloistered pity go
To find the wells of charity,
    Since Thou hast loved us so?

III

O Holy Spirit, Thou best Gift
    Sent down from Heaven above,
May Thy sweet inspirations lift
    Our lives to deeds of love.

AT THE CLOSE OF SERVICE

I

O HOLY One,
  Our prayers are done,
And with Thy blessing may our worship cease.
  To all that waits
 Beyond the shelter of Thy gates
Now lettest Thou Thy servants go in peace.

II

O Glorious One,
Our songs are done;
The world is calling and its cares increase.
  With lips that praise
 And hearts that softly sing always,
Now lettest Thou Thy servants go in peace.

At the Close of Service

III

O Changeless One,
When life is done
Breathe through the dark Thy pardon and release.
Thou wilt forget,
But lest some shame may linger yet,
Now lettest Thou Thy servants go in peace.

Hymns from the Latin

1

**O luce qui mortalibus
Lates inaccessa, Deus!
Praesente quo sancti tremunt
Nubuntque vultus angeli.**

(*By* CHARLES COFFIN; *born 1676, died 1749. In the Paris Breviary of 1736 it is the hymn appointed for Vespers on the Sundays from Trinity to Advent.*)

I

O GOD Most High,
By mortal eye
Unseen, Thou hidest in the light,
Upon whose brink
E'en angels shrink,
And veil their faces from the sight.

II

'Tis darkness here,
And, far or near,
Through deepest shadow lies the way
Unto the gate,—
And there to wait
The rising of eternal day.

O luce qui mortalibus

III

The flash of dawn
So quickly gone,
The brightest blaze of noontide's ray,
Like twilight seem
Beside the gleam
And glory of that coming day.

IV

O golden day,
So far away,
Why dost thou linger, yet how long?
From flesh set free
The soul must be
Ere it can join thy morning song.

V

Its chains put by,
How swift to fly,
O God, to look upon Thy face!
Of love to Thee
Its song shall be,
Its lasting joy to praise Thy grace.

O luce qui mortalibus

VI

Blest Trinity,
May Thy gifts be
Our gracious helpers by the way,
Till our brief night
Shall catch the light
That heralds the eternal day.

O Christe, qui noster poli
Praecursor intras regiam,
Quos hic jacentes respicis,
Sursum voca, sursum rape.

(*A hymn first appearing in the Cluniac Breviary of 1686.*)

I

OUR Herald-Christ at Heaven's gate,
    Our King within its walls,
Thine eye yet sees us, lingering late;
    Thy voice, once more it calls.

II

Make us to seek with love more bold
    Those joys that purer seem,
Which earthly eyes may not behold,
    Nor faith's, except in dream.

III

Where hearts that strove yet feared to fall,
    And hands that toiled, have rest;
Where God Himself is All-in-all,
    And all His own are blest.

O Christe, qui noster poli

IV

And lest we lose that glory's crown,
    And lest we miss that prize,
O Christ, Thy Spirit's grace send down
    To give us strength to rise.

V

All praise to Thee, our Herald-King,
    With Him at whose right hand
Thou art, and Him whose power can bring
    Thy children to that land.

Crux ave benedicta!
Per te mors est devicta,
In te dependit Deus,
Rex et Salvator meus.

(*A passion hymn of unknown authorship.*)

I

HAIL, blessed cross! Those arms of thine
    Have drawn from death its sting,
For they have borne the Lord Divine,
    My Saviour and my King.

II

Of all earth's trees the queenliest,
    Of all earth's ills the cure,
Of burdened hearts thou art the rest,
    Of griefs, the solace sure.

III

O holiest wood! the pledge and sign
    Of our new life thou art;
And on thee grows the fruit Divine
    That feeds the human heart.

Crux ave benedicta!

IV

When those that love and those that hate
   Thy cross shall summoned be,
O Jesus, for whose call they wait,
   I pray, remember me.

Nobis, Olympo redditus,
Qui, Christe, sedes praeparas,
Nos exules in patriam
Trahas amoris nexibus.

(*An Ascension Hymn, by* Jean-Baptiste de Santeüil; *born 1630, died 1697. I have taken the text from the second edition of his* Hymni Sacri et Novi, Paris, 1698, *in preference to that of the Paris Breviary, which omits the second verse and adds a somewhat inconsequent doxology.*)

I

RETURNED to Heaven and reigning there,
Our place, O Christ, Thou dost prepare:
Now gently draw with cords of love
Thine exiles to their home above,

II

Where dwell the blest, from cares how free,
Secure in their felicity;
And there at life's full river's brink
Deep draughts of bliss immortal drink.

Nobis, Olympo redditus

III

With all good gifts abounding, Lord,
Thou shalt be there our great Reward:
Beside those pleasures which remain,
How brief this passing day of pain!

IV

And when the veil is drawn apart,
And we behold Thee as Thou art,
Our love shall answer Thine always,
Our lips shall never cease Thy praise.

V

Till then be mindful of Thine own,
And, like a dove from far heights flown,
The Spirit of adoption send
To pledge our welcome at the end.

Ter sancte, ter potens Deus,
Incomprehensa Trinitas:
O lux perennis! propriis
O ter beata gaudiis!

(*By* Claude de Santeüil; *born 1628, died 1684. The hymn is
assigned to Trinity Sunday in the Paris Breviary.*)

I

THRICE-HOLY God, of threefold might,
    The Trinity confessed,
Thrice-glorious with eternal light,
    With joys Divine thrice-blest!

II

O Unity forever true,
    O Truth forever one,
Eternal Love forever new,
    Whose gifts are never done!

III

Thick clouds of darkness like a wall
    Conceal Thy splendor's blaze,
Where angels on their faces fall,
    Nor, trembling, dare to gaze.

Ter sancte, ter potens Deus

IV

Thy flock sounds forth Thy threefold Name
   In which it is baptized;
Faith sights the Heaven from which it came,
   And love would grasp the prize.

V

Lord, give us grace to do Thy will;
   O Christ, instruct the heart;
Thou Holy Spirit, help us still
   To choose the better part.

VI

Let God the Father be adored,
   With his coequal Son,
And with the Holy Ghost, one Lord,
   Thrice-royal, ever One.

**Nil laudibus nostris eges,
Sed filios amas, Pater;
Multaque coelestem prece
Vis provocari gratiam.**

By CHARLES COFFIN; *born 1676, died 1749. Like most of his hymns, this one first appeared in the Paris Breviary of 1736, where it is appointed for Monday at Lauds.*)

I

OUR praises, Lord, Thou dost not need;
   'Tis rather that Thy love
Would have Thy children come to plead
   For blessings from above.

II

The secrets of Thy dark decrees
   Deep night in silence sings;
Thy mercy's light, in golden seas,
   The flooding sunshine brings.

III

Nor thought nor voice fulfil their part,
   When by such wonders thrilled;
Yet love that pulses through the heart
   Refuses to be stilled.

Nil laudibus nostris eges

IV

So let it speak our Father's praise
    To Thee, whose grace affords
A present help in evil days,
    And hope of great rewards.

V

To them our dearest wishes rise,
    Though earthly thoughts contend:
O Jesus, draw us toward the skies,
    And guide us till the end.

O Pater sancte mitis atque pie,
O Jesu Christe Fili venerande,
Paracliteque Spiritus O alme,
    Deus aeterne.

(A hymn of unknown authorship found in more than one manuscript of the eleventh century.)

I

FATHER, all-holy, merciful, and tender,
    Christ, fitly worshipped in Thy royal splendor,
Spirit most gracious, Helper and Defender,
    God everlasting!

II

Trinity holy, Unity unbroken,
God, of whose greatness goodness is the token,
Joy of the angels, Balm of griefs unspoken,
    Hope all-surpassing!

III

All things to serve Thee, Lord, Thou hast created;
All creatures' homage, Lord, on Thee has waited;
Our hymns we offer, to Thee dedicated:
    Hear them ascending.

O Pater sancte mitis atque pie

IV

Glory to Thee, O Sovereign God Almighty,
Whose power and greatness Three-in-One unite
    Thee;
Anthems and praises unto Thee most rightly
    Rise never ending.

𝔇eus, 𝔓ater ingenite,
𝔈t 𝔉ili unigenite,
𝔔uos 𝔗rinitatis unitas
𝔖ancto connectit 𝔖piritu.

(*By* HILARY OF POICTIERS, *who died at that place A.D. 368. His hymns, but few of which have survived, stand among the beginnings of Latin Hymnody.*)

I

FATHER unbegotten,
    Sole-begotten Son,
With the Holy Spirit,
    God the Three-in-One;

II

Never one who seeks Thee
    Breathes a futile prayer:
When love's face is lifted,
    Heaven's light falls there.

III

Hear, O God, the voices
    Paying vows to Thee;
To their hearts' confessions
    Ever gracious be.

Deus, Pater ingenite

IV

Now the dawn reminds us
  Of the thanks we owe,
Wakens songs of praises
  As the shadows go.

V

Hear us, Gracious Saviour,
  Hallow this new day,
Order all our doings,
  Lest our footsteps stray.

Salvator mundi, Domine,
Qui nos salvasti hodie,
In hac nocte nos protege,
Et salva omni tempore.

(*A hymn of unknown authorship which* Mone *thinks of the sixth or seventh century. It is found in several hymnaries and breviaries, where it seems to have no fixed place, but is assigned to varying seasons of the Church year.*)

I

O THOU, the Saviour of the world,
    Who kept us safe to-day,
Through all this night protect us still,
    And save us, Lord, alway.

II

Reveal Thy gracious presence now,
    And spare us while we pray;
Lift off the burden of our sins,
    And turn our night to day.

Salvator mundi, Domine

III

May sleep fall lightly on the soul,
  No sudden foe surprise,
Nor any stain defile the flesh
  While it unguarded lies.

IV

To Thee, Renewer of our lives,
  Our earnest prayer we make,
That we serene and pure in heart
  From out of sleep may wake.

V

To God the Father glory be
  And to His only Son,
With God the Holy Comforter,
  Forever Three-in-One.

[The hymns at pages 18 and 64 are reprinted here by kind permission of the Editor of The Sunday School Times, wherein they first appeared.]

Verses

THE BELLS OF CHRIST CHURCH

OVER the roofs that rise between
    I hear the bells of Christ Church chiming;
  As though upon bright hills unseen
Glad angels sang where they were climbing,
  Or some stray minstrel, passing by,
Carolled his airy fancies, rhyming,
  That laughed together in the sky,
And set the bells of Christ Church chiming.

  Above the clamor of the town
I hear the bells of Christ Church ringing;
  As though some herald, flying down,
His messages of peace were bringing,
  And all the voices of the air
In sweet companionship were singing
  The call to worship and to prayer
In Christ Church, where the bells are ringing.

The Bells of Christ Church

    Out of the darkness and the rain
I hear the bells of Christ Church tolling;
    As though long rhythmic waves of pain
Upon a cloudland shore were rolling,
    Where some sad spirit, left alone,
In need of friendship and consoling,
    Counted his sorrows one by one.
I hear the bells of Christ Church tolling.

1882.

LITTLE FOOT ON THE FENDER

'TIS a little song that I send her;
   'Tis a little maid whom I see;
'Tis a little foot on the fender,
   And a prayer,—will it wait for me?

May the angels of God attend her,
   Who are nearer than I can be;
And thou, little foot on the fender,
   Wilt thou walk the long path with me?

THE LAST HILL

(A painting by James Hamilton.)

UP from low valleys where the slow brooks wind
    Between the meadow lands, with wavering wills
That hear the sea, yet love the haunts behind,
    Starts the long path of life across the hills.

Now lies the glow of morning on the path,
    With borders of wild blossom laid along;
Its first found upland greeted with a laugh,
    Its easy summits mounted with a song.

With lavish life the fields and woods are green,
    'Neath radiant skies that arch the perfect days;
And many are the friends we walk between,
    Before we reach the parting of the ways,

Where every path is waiting for its own,
    Inviting him to come, he sees not where,
Save only when the boughs, asunder blown,
    Reveal far summits in the distant air.

The Last Hill

And now, with all his comrades laid at rest
   In backward valleys, where they linger still,
This lonely pilgrim at the utmost west
   Has reached the sloping crown of life's last hill.

He wades among the drifted autumn leaves
   With his worn staff, and peers with vacant sight
Into the dim beyond, where sunset weaves
   A faded border on the edge of night,

Which on the caps of cloud-hills lingers last,—
   The glow of hope that vanishes in pain
Off airy summits rising from the past,
   Far gleaming, so long toiled for, unattained.

Do joys remembered seem to fall again,
   From off long-withered seasons, at the sight
Of frosted foliage dropping like the rain
   From swaying boughs left naked to the night?

And does he hear again the fall of feet
   That somewhere, sometime, in the long ago,
Kept pace with his, when carelessly and fleet
   They trod the glad hills, flushed with eastern glow?

The Last Hill

And do their voices, over hills between,
   Sound faintly still, like cries of passing flocks,
Or as through trees, from cataracts unseen,
   Come sounds of falling waters on the rocks?

They do not rise from out the valley there
   To greet him now; they come not with the breeze,
Out of the dusk, that tosses his white hair,
   And shivers in the branches of bare trees.

Louder the night-wind wails about the hill;
   Deeper the shadows gather over him;
Forgetful happily, and dreaming still,
   He disappears into the unknown dim

By paths our human foresight may not trace,
   Across th' untrodden valley of the west,
And over brightening hills, to that fair place
   Where lies, beyond the pilgrimage, our rest.

   1878.

ON LAKE GEORGE

ON the dreamy waters drifting,
    Hills around me and before,
While the moon the veil is lifting
    From the islands and the shore.

Dreaming, drifting; drifting, dreaming;
    Sipping draughts of airy lore
From the fount of fancy streaming
    On the islands and the shore.

Dreams — they rise with sweet persistence
    From the dim and mists of yore,
Rise and pass into the distance
    With the islands and the shore.

Oh, to drift and dream forever!
    Oh, to drift for evermore
On a tide of dreams that never
    Laps an island or a shore!

1879.

MY FATHER'S HOUSE

LIKE songs resung, yet seeming not the same,
    I hear soft notes of laughter; and a voice,
Clearer than other voices, calls my name
    From out the silence of my father's house.

Like cloudy highlands lifted from the night,
    Yet golden in the lingering afterglow,
Arise remembered seasons, and a light
    That lifts the shadows in my father's house.

Intangible, yet beautiful, they seem,
    Like glimpses of things longed for from afar;
And I, as one that waketh from a dream
    That framed the fabric of my father's house.

When still I join with other hands mine own,
    They thrill and falter with unspoken thought,
So strangely smaller has the circle grown,
    So strangely empty is my father's house.

My Father's House

Oh, vacant chamber and untrodden hall,
   And things familiar that have lost their use!
Oh, days of meeting and of festival
   That were so merry in my father's house!

I may not linger, and I turn away;
   Hush, now, ye solemn voices of the night!
Lo! glimmers from the east another day
   Against the portals of my Father's House.

1883.

"AND THERE SHALL BE NO NIGHT THERE"

THERE'S a red burst of dawn, and a white light of noon,
  [And the hues of the rainbow are seven;]
But the best thing of all, when the dark comes so soon,
  Is to know that it's ne'er night in Heaven.

There's a break in the clouds, and a sheen on the rain,
  [And the hues of the rainbow are seven;]
But the sweetest of lights that can brighten our pain
  Is to know that it's ne'er night in Heaven.

There's a calm of the heart through the long afternoon,
  [And the gifts of the Spirit are seven,]
When there floats on the dusk, like a leaf-whispered tune,
  " Did you know that it's ne'er night in Heaven?"

"And There Shall Be No Night There"

There's a gleam through the night of a throne set afar,
  [And the hues of its rainbow are seven;]
But it stands not so sure as God's promises are,
  Who has said, "There is no night in Heaven."

AN AUCTION

ONE little maid in a cradle,
    Two little maids in a bed;
Three little heads laid together,
    Two little prayers softly said.
"Just a last kiss," comes from Sister,
    And a "Me, too," from the bed;
Never a sound from the cradle,
    One little prayer still unsaid.

One little maid and a cradle,
    Two little maids and a bed;
Three little maids altogether,
    Offered at so much per head.
What will you give me for Sister?
    What for Me Too on the bed?
What am I bid for the baby?
    Going, at so much per head.

An Auction

WHAT! for the babe, or the cradle?
   WHAT! But you mean for the bed?
WHAT! 'Will I start with the baby?'
   Sir, did I catch what you said?
Gentlemen all, name your figures
   Either for cradle or bed;
But — did I mention a limit
   Placed on each dear little head?

AN AFTERNOON IN NOVEMBER

SINCE Nellie strayed through autumn woods,
    Where would you have her lover?
She sat upon a fallen tree,
    And I bent down above her.

It seemed a sunny afternoon,
    Although it was November;
But if 'twas warm or if 'twas cold,
    I really can't remember.

Somehow her little heart and mine
    Seemed just so close together,
Perhaps there was no room between
    For any sort of weather.

I trembled at her coy dismay
    As I leaned down above her,
Until I looked in her brown eyes,
    And then I said I loved her.

An Afternoon in November

So sweetly then the dearest smile
   Played softly through her blushes,
So precious the low words between
   Her shy and dreamy hushes, —

That when I told my story through,
   How long I'd been her lover,
I took her little hand in mine,
   And straightway told it over.

I must not write what Nellie said : —
   Old book, you just remember
That, if the crops are good, there'll be
   A wedding in November.

THE PRAISE OF PENN
1882

(The two hundredth anniversary of his landing.)

NOT with the trumpet blast of martial song,
    The noisy minstrelsy
And plaudits that to conquerors belong,
    The praise of Penn shall be;
But simple words from hearts that love the right
    Shall greet the man of peace,
Whose name, enduring yet, shall glow more bright
    When sounds of war shall cease.

The woods unfurled to the October air
    Pennons of gold and flame,
When, sailing up the river Delaware,
    The good ship Welcome came;
And all who dwelt upon its fertile banks,
    Dutch, Swedes, and Englishmen,
Gave salutation, unto God their thanks,
    And their right hands to Penn.

The Praise of Penn

Two hundred times upon the Delaware
    The autumn leaves, since then,
Have drifted seaward; and the dwellers there
    Who gave their hands to Penn
Long since are mingled with the leaves. No more
    The Welcome sails the sea,
Forever harbored by the sheltering shore
    Of the heart's loyalty.

Yet now, two hundred autumns afterward,
    The woods in red and gold,
And, stately as its founder's dream restored,
    The city he foretold,
The broad fields stretching outward to the sea
    Along the river-shore,
Wait at the portals of a century
    To welcome Penn once more.

And what of thee? O woodland commonwealth!
    O commonwealth of Penn!
That art no more a woodland, but a breadth
    Of empire. Standing then,
In woods unbroken to the northern lake,
    Thy forest trees; so all
Thy sons, as many, stand, who for thy sake
    Like forest trees would fall.

The Praise of Penn

Thou, from thy reverend altitude of days,
    With hand uplifted now,
Dost bind two woven centuries of praise
    About thy founder's brow;
While loyal millions, loving him and thee,
    Pledge in their hearts' red wine
Two names, made one in holy unity
    Forever — his and thine.

Not with the trumpet blast of martial song,
    The noisy minstrelsy
And plaudits that to conquerors belong,
    The praise of Penn shall be;
But rather in our watchfulness for thee,
    O queenly State! our prayer
That civil peace and the soul's liberty
    May dwell immortal there.

MEMORY

A HILL that fronts a headland to the sea
    Booming beneath and stretching endlessly;
      An edge of land
      Where bushes wind-swept grow,
    And stunted trees that budded stand,
      Yet hesitate to blow;
    And from the hill, shadowed and black,
      The herald of the dawn,
    Not yet announced, looks back,
      His trumpet still withdrawn,
As though he had forgotten to forget,
Or something to the dawn were lacking yet.

FAMILIAR MUSIC

HEAR, through the summer night, voices of boatmen
   Singing the melodies they love the best,
Launched in the passing airs, rippling, that float them
   Far into distance and harbors of rest.

How all the placid night thrills into music,
   As when, in brightening woods, birds are awake!
Softly, from either shore, the hills refuse it
   In timid whispers that die on the lake.

Now ye come nearer me, boatmen, yet nearer;
   Louder the rhythmical plash of the oar:
Rest there a little while, a lonely hearer
   Paces in silence, and unseen, the shore.

Boatmen, ye sing to him songs of his childhood,
   Though in a tongue he cannot understand;
Dear as familiar flowers found in the wildwood,
   They, to a stranger, and in a strange land.

Familiar Music

Tears overcoming me, tears of remembrance
   Mingle your music with songs heard before.
Ah! your companionship was but a semblance;
   Ye have rowed past me; I hear you no more.

1882.

THE OLD LOVES AND THE NEW

I LOVE old books of wholesome wit
    In calf-skin (why rebind them?);
For though with fun their sides have split,
    They leave a smile behind them:
And some new books,—the Autocrat's
    (Saucy! you must not mind them);
Birrell, his dicta; Lang, his chats;
    'And Smiles?' The smiles behind them.

I love old friends (some added grace
    Could scarcely have refined them)
That say they love you to your face
    When you have wined and dined them:
And some new friends. The old are best
    If one could only find them.
(Don't go! Your smiles are the bequest
    The old ones left behind them.)

The Old Loves and the New

I love true eyes, the time o' day
    When love has undermined them
(Just turn your face, my dear, this way)
    By smiles that lurk behind them.
I love bright eyes — (you scamp), I'd dare
    With kisses now to blind them
But that two imps of mischief there
    Would surely have declined them.

A NOONING

OH, this is rest, — to lie beside
    The little woodland stream,
To watch the silvered waters slide
Down mossy rocks, then gently glide
    Through shadow and sunbeam.

And like a bird that finds his mate,
    And poises melodies
Upon the boughs, I meditate
On love, and freely cultivate
    The comradeship of trees.

Some other day, some otherwhere,
    I dream, as I lie here,
Wait fields unploughed that need the share,
From sun to sun the round of care,
    The toil, the pain, the tear.

1878.

TO-MORROW

AN old strain (which poets borrow)
    Sings that "Sorrow's crown of sorrow
Is remembering happier days."
But the blackest robe of sorrow
Is the shadow of to-morrow
    And to-morrow and always.

THE TEMPLE OF THE NEW JERUSALEM

(UPPER DARBY, PENNSYLVANIA.)

THE Summer wears her crown
   On this the thirtieth morning of the May:
Proudly the Sun looks down
Upon his new-born child, a golden day.

   Here the wild grasses wave,
And summer blossoms that elsewhere are laid
   On many a soldier's grave
With martial ceremony and parade.

   Beside the quiet lane
That winds among the farms on either hand,
   Meadows and fields of grain,
The little church of Swedenborg doth stand,

   Far from the beating heart
Of the world's business and activity;
   From all its ways apart
In unpretentious, quaint simplicity.

The Temple of the New Jerusalem

    The trees that border it
Have mystic shadows interweaving them,
    And o'er the door is writ,
"The Temple of the New Jerusalem."

    Sweet as a saintly face
The simple faith that did not hesitate,
    Nor deem it strange, to place
Upon so small a house a name so great.

    In these bare walls, perchance,
It saw the symbol of a temple here
    Not built by human hands,
But vaster, holier, as when angels rear,

    Upon a living rock,
A fabric spiritual of living stones,
    Such as a little flock
Like this may offer of God's chosen ones.

    Closed is the door; and I
Tread the secluded place of graves, and muse
    On the unknown who lie
Beneath, once wont to occupy these pews.

The Temple of the New Jerusalem

This is their family home,
Of which the church seems but the vestibule,
And hither they are come
Like tired children hurrying from school.

Here is the pastor's grave,
His faithful flock beside him gathered still:
He powerless to save,
And they to follow up the heavenly hill.

Yonder I read his name,
Who in these colonies of old King George,
First, for his master's fame,
Printed the mystic words of Swedenborg.

A tiny flag I see
Over a soldier's grave, as if in prayer
It waved its hand to me,
To stoop and lay these starry daisies there.

I thought I was alone;
But there, beside the unmarked mound of clay,
An aged form bends down
To celebrate her Decoration Day.

The Temple of the New Jerusalem

So womanhood doth bow
At many shrines deserted but by her;
   The last to hope, and now
She lingers last beside the sepulchre.

   I leave her with her own;
And fancy I were satisfied to know
   That, when my years have flown,
I, too, might lie in peace where wild flowers grow;

   To wake, beyond the years,
With these that slept, a worshipper with them
   When in the Heavens appears
The Temple of the New Jerusalem.

1882.

Sonnets

BRYANT

1878

O POET, in whose song we heard the breath
    Of winds through woodlands musical with
        birds,
    And sounds of falling waters in thy words,
    Why is it, when thou liest low in death,
The earth thou didst so love can bear to be
    Apparelled in the cheerfulness of June?
    The arc thou sawest groweth to full-moon,
    Nor doth all nature mould one tear for thee:

But in our hearts a still of autumn broods,
    And there, in sad and dreamy undertone,
    Thy scarce-hushed voice, remembered, lingers still
Like sobbings of a wind through frost-shorn woods
    When from bared boughs the singing-birds have
        flown,
    And withered leaves are drifting down the hill.

A DEDICATION

THIS simple offering that I may not send
    To whom I would, with love I consecrate,
  And, on her altar laid, I dedicate
These verses to the memory of my friend.
Time wrote them on my heart, and I but lend
    A voice to sing them, while beyond my sight
    He somewhere waits till time "The end" shall write
Beneath my verses, and restore my friend.

Time wrote them in the twilight that must be
    In this our lasting friendship's way-side inn,
    Since God so suddenly put out the light
That showed the features of his face to me,
    And took His wondering boy away with Him
Ere he had time to bid me a Good-night.

    10th February, 1881.

LONELINESS

I HEARD a plaintive sound among the trees,
  A breath of murmured music, and a throb
That, if it had been human, were a sob,
And died away in sighings on the breeze.
Then in my heart I said, "Within this wood
  There is a sympathy: kind nature weaves
  About my grief a coronal of leaves,
And binds it with a song of saddest mood."

Ah, no! It is the soul alone that grieves;
  And never yet our sorrows wrung a sigh
  From nature, but our fancy woke to find
We heard but rhythmic rustlings of the leaves,
  That flap and twist and bend unpityingly
  Beneath the pulseless fingers of the wind.

1881.

THE UNCHANGEABLE

HOW beautiful the thought to one who stands
    Encircled by a tidal-flow of change,
  Whose billows, with a murmur sad and strange,
  Break ceaselessly about him on the sands;
While chilly-burdened winds encompassing
    The shore, make monody of days that were,
  With prophecies of all unrest, and stir
  His soul with longing for some steadfast thing:—

How beautiful to him the thought of God,
    Who, farther back than cycle-reach, was Love,
  And shall be when the cycles die again,
Still Love, unchangeable: a shore so broad,
    So firm, beyond all tides, all storms above,
  A rock 'gainst which time-billows dash in vain!

    1878.

CEDARS BY MOONLIGHT

(*An etching by* SMILLIE.)

A GROUP of cedars rising from a hill,
   Spectral, distinct, against the mottled sky:
  Above them, through the thin clouds sailing by,
  The moon shines timidly, against its will.
And they are clustered close, as though a thrill
   Of fear possessed them that they were so high
   Upon the mountain-ridge, the edge so nigh,
  The vault beyond so fathomless and still:—

I know not where. Perchance it only be
   The mind's remembrance of some halting-place,
   Wherein, beneath hope's fitful gleams, I stood;
Yet half afraid, because I could not see
   Its light reflected from some other face,
  Nor through the moonless shadows find the road.

1882.

OF THEM THAT SLEEP

OF you, our hearts' beloved, who are dead,
    I, who have stayed behind you, softly sing;
  Sing softly, as the wind does, murmuring
  Among the trees for blossoms that are shed,
And all the summer greenness that has fled;
    In its own wind's way quaintly questioning
    Why all the leaves that budded in the spring
  Have fallen, and are drifting, restless, dead.

I sing, and can ye hear me? And do I
    Hear nothing, while I listen, but the wind
    For something seeking that it cannot find,
And calling, vainly calling, passing by?
    My heart cries to the distance, and says Hark!
    As one that heard an echo through the dark.

1882.

The March of Braddock

THE MARCH OF BRADDOCK
1755

THE wind that blew from westward, like a courier mounted well,
Sped o'er the Alleghanies with the news it had to tell
From inn to inn by every road, at every farm and forge,
To every loyal subject of His Majesty King George
Between Savannah River and the waters of Champlain:—
"The lilies of the Bourbon King wave over Fort Du Quesne."

It bore the news to England, like a carrier strong of wing,
And whispered it in Cabinet to Cumberland and King.
They summon General Braddock: "You a trusty soldier are;
Take our two Irish regiments of Halket and Dunbar
Across the sea, and fight the French with all your might and main,
And bring you back that Bourbon rag, torn down from Fort Du Quesne."

The March of Braddock

The wind that blew from eastward brought an English fleet to shore,
The Norwich, the Centurion, transports and ships of store.
At Yorktown and St. Mary's, too, it was a joyful day
When like a flock of water-birds they sailed up Chesapeake Bay.
"Hurrah for General Braddock!" and again and yet again,
"God speed the British Regulars who march to Fort Du Quesne!"

Toward camp at Alexandria the provincial levies come
To the shrill blast of the fifers and the beating of the drum,—
The hatchetmen and carpenters, the rangers and light-horse;
And underneath their uniforms, motley and quaint and coarse,
Their honest hearts are panting for the glory they shall gain
In the service of old Braddock and the conquest of Du Quesne.

The March of Braddock

'Loud laugh the Regulars to see the raw militia boys,
Who gave themselves ('twas all they had) to help the royal cause,
But did not wear their throbbing hearts upon their homespun sleeves.
To Governor Dinwiddie, "Pray, what sort of troops are these?"
Exclaims the pompous General in the shock of his disdain.
"Well, General, you may need them ere you get to Fort Du Quesne."

O weary months of waiting in the half-provisioned camp,
The General with the Governors around the council-lamp:
He fumes and storms above them, and he shakes before their eyes
Their pledges and their contracts for his waggons and supplies.
He curses them, their colonies; the Governors explain:
And still the Bourbon lilies wave o'er distant Fort Du Quesne.

The March of Braddock

The spring is green before his troops begin to move away;
The spring has turned to summer-time before their full array
Is mustered at Fort Cumberland, and their commander's eyes
See all made ready for the march beneath the burning skies.
Hark! There's the signal cannon in the clear air sounding plain;
"Fall in" and "Forward march" at last, and off for Fort Du Quesne!

Straight up the pathless mountain-range they push their devious course,
Artillery and infantry, the waggons and light-horse;
St. Clair ahead; the struggling line trails back of him four miles,
A living thread stretched ready to be snapped by savage wiles;
The horses broken-kneed, the men are sick with heat and pain:
A hundred thirty miles away as yet is Fort Du Quesne.

The March of Braddock

'Into Great Savage Wilderness the axemen cut their way
Through towering forests of white pine that bar the light of day,
Within whose gloomy silence lives no creature that has breath;
And man to man is whispering, "They are called The Shades of Death."
Hark! Firing there! The Indians? 'Tis some horse in mercy slain.
And with each sinking sun they gain but two miles toward Du Quesne.

The cannon and the waggons, some are spiked and some are broke,
And some get down the precipice with tackle and with rope.
Now lash the panting horses! and now cheer the fainting men!
The cliffs of Meadow Mountain must be climbed to-day: and then
Behold the Little Meadows, for St. Clair has gained the plain:
His camp is but a hundred miles away from Fort Du Quesne.

The March of Braddock

Now halt till the pack-horses and the waggons come in slow;
Halt here for Major Washington (he gave out long ago):
Now halt until the stragglers come with bruisèd, bleeding feet,
And deal them out an extra share of water and salt meat:
Halt for Dunbar the Tardy,—and the equinoctial rain
Will fall before the British flag is planted on Du Quesne.

Forward the light division! The four hundred with St. Clair;
And where they make a forest path, Braddock will follow there;
Through streams and deep morasses, over mountain and through glen,
To where man's foot has never trod, go forward, Englishmen!
The sun shall dry your bleeding feet, the showers cool your brain,
As, tracked by skulking savages, you march to Fort Du Quesne.

The March of Braddock

The last hard climb is over, and the last day's setting sun
Glares red upon the camping-ground by wild Sewickley Run;
Between the netted foliage there its latest wavering gleam
Is flashed from the fresh-burnished arms stacked close beside the stream,
And every tired soldier on the ground where he has lain
Is dreaming that to-morrow night he sleeps in Fort Du Quesne.

Thy shores, Monongahela, see a royal sight this day
When Braddock with his Regulars in their full-dress array,
To bursts of martial melody from every hill retold,
Thy shallows ford; their uniforms of scarlet and of gold
Within thy waves reflected till the sloping banks they gain,
And rally with an English cheer that's heard at Fort Du Quesne.

The March of Braddock

"The road is open, General: 'tis an easy path from here."
"Then forward, boys, one effort more: now one more English cheer!"
"Hold! hold!" pleads cautious Washington; "make sure beyond a doubt;
Let the Virginian foresters go beat these woods about."
"You raw militia stripling, if you're afraid you can remain,"
Old Braddock says, and swears an oath he'll sup in Fort Du Quesne.

"Forward!" the angry General shouts: quickly his troops reply.
Up from the river-bank they come; "We're almost there," they cry.
Beat louder, faster, drummers! while they march with eager stride
Into the narrow forest road, hemmed in on either side;
Looking to see the fort ahead at each turn of the lane,
And not an enemy in sight between them and Du Quesne.

The March of Braddock

Firing upon the front! and now the charging cheers of troops,
The thrilling "Vive le Roi!" amid blood-curdling Indian whoops.
Firing along the wavering lines! and now upon the rear
Still standing firm and waiting till the enemy appear!
Like hail the balls and arrows come; like dead leaves fall the slain;
But not an enemy in sight between them and Du Quesne.

The advance gives way, the regiments are herded into one;
While to the forefront Braddock rides, his charger at full run:
"Around your colours rally, men: now forward by platoons:"
Waving his sword above his head, the wounded General swoons.
Across his body where he lies, now kicked and kicked again,
The panting herd of soldiers rush at full run from Du Quesne!

The March of Braddock

Fly, fly, ye British Regulars: throw down your arms and fly,
And leave your fallen General on the battle-field to die;
Across the ford and through the woods to camp, and tell Dunbar
That dead and dying in the road eight hundred soldiers are!
Fly, fly, ye British Regulars, with all your might and main;
The Indians chase, — fly faster than you came to Fort Du Quesne!

But of the horrors of that scene when all who could have flown,
And to the Indians left the rest — the death-shriek and the groan,
The savage torture limb by limb — no human voice could tell,
Though it should speak with cloven tongues of fire from deepest hell.
Shame! shame to France, — the eyes that look, the hands that might restrain!
And in the setting sun blush red her lilies on Du Quesne.

The March of Braddock

O night-wind from the westward, passing over Braddock's Field,
Thou needst not pray the shadows there his mangled corpse to shield.
By brave Virginia soldiers, and on strong Virginia arms,
He's borne beyond the scalpers' reach and fear of their alarms;
The death-sweat on his forehead, while he whispers, in his pain,
To lay him in a nameless grave not far from Fort Du Quesne.

O night-wind, speed from inn to inn, to every farm and forge,
To every anxious subject of His Majesty King George:
Awaken Philadelphia with thy blasts untimely cold,
And from the steeple of Christ Church let muffled bells be tolled;
While yet the voice that trembles through the names of brave men slain
Thanks Heaven that saved Washington from death at Fort Du Quesne.

The March of Braddock

O wind that blows from westward, waft the ship in which he came
Who sends back nothing to his King except a tarnished name:
Tell out thy tale at council-board: the Duke himself shall say,
"Had Washington commanded, there were better news to-day."
Blow, blow, ye winds from westward, till your warnings shall make plain
The lesson God taught England by defeat at Fort Du Quesne.

1880.

www.ingramcontent.com/pod-product-compliance
Lightning Source LLC
Chambersburg PA
CBHW021940160426
43195CB00011B/1162